The People They Knew

Elegies, Dedications, and Other Poems

Dr. Calvin D. Franklin

Dr. Bryant,
Thank you for being you!
& Thank you for being
good ground! God Bless
— Dr. C. Franklin

A wholly owned subsidiary of **TBN**

The People They Knew

Trilogy Christian Publishers A Wholly Owned Subsidiary of Trinity Broadcasting Network

2442 Michelle Drive Tustin, CA 92780

Manufactured in the United States of America

10 9 8 7 6 5 4 3 2 1

Library of Congress Cataloging-in-Publication Data is available.

ISBN: 978-1-68556-127-7

E-ISBN: 978-1-68556-128-4

Dedication

"How can I say thanks for the things that you have done for me? Things so undeserved yet you gave to prove your love for me; the voices of a million angels could not express my gratitude. All that I am and ever hope to be, I owe it all to you. To God be the glory. To God be the glory. To God be the glory for the things He has done."

—Andrae Crouch

Acknowledgments

Thank you to all the bereaved families who allowed me to elegize their loved ones and to share in the celebration of the lives they shared with so many. I appreciate being able to participate in memorializing them. My prayer is that the elegies, dedications, etc., will serve to comfort you as you remember your loved ones for the years to come and that the generations after you will be able to catch a glimpse of the people you knew who have transitioned from this life.

I'd also like to thank everyone who allowed me to be a part of your accomplishments and gave me the liberty to express my sentiments toward who you are and who I perceive you to be.

In Loving Memory of The People They Knew

Sunset, Sunrise

There, the sun sets on my tomorrows

No suns past or present from which I can borrow

And as the rays retreat and dim

Eternity's dawn erases my sorrows

Eternity

My sorrows erased with my earthly tomorrows.

O, how great the mourning and weeping

For my comforts are mute to you who are seeking

But let the tears turn to dancing

Your rejoicing lifts me into heavenly leaping

Rejoice

Rejoicing will lift the mourning and weeping

Yes, the gulping grave is cold and hard

Only He finally escaped that bitter, lonely yard

But as the ground seals its mouth

Pearly Gates open to Blessed Boulevard
Pearly Gates
Open gates close the grave, cold and hard

Now, endure when it seems you're all alone
Though my hand is absent to ease your soul's groan
And before you even think
Together, all of His will be around the throne
Together
We'll be at His throne, nevermore alone.

Table of Contents

Introduction

In July of 2009, a man by the name of Frank Powell, Sr., passed from this life into the next. I had never met Mr. Powell. In fact, I knew nothing about him except that his daughter was a coworker of mine and that she was mourning his death. She and I were not particularly acquainted. We only shared cordial greetings and workspace. However, the fact that she was mourning the loss of her father touched me, and I was moved to do something to help comfort her in her time of loss.

I had written poems before but never had I written an elegy. The word "elegy" was not even in my vocabulary. However, upon notice of Mr. Powell's passing, I decided that a mere greeting card was insufficient for the condolences that I wished to send for the occasion. So, I began to write a poem specially dedicated in loving memory of Mr. Frank Powell, Sr. I was sure to frame the poem and see that my coworker received it.

Upon returning to work, I was met with a thankful embrace and words of gratitude for my special gift. I was elated that my gift had conveyed sincere condolences to a grieving family and that the condolences were well received. The poem that led to this exchange became the beginning of what is now a body of work that I've decided to share with as many as would take the time to read and enjoy it. Thank you to the late Mr. Frank Powell, Sr. It all started with him.

Over the years, I have begun to intentionally memorialize people and special moments with words that I hoped would leave lasting impressions on the readers and hearers. Communication through words has become extremely important to me. As the great Dr. Maya Angelou expressed, *"I've learned that people will forget what you said, people will forget what you did, but people will never forget how you made them feel."*

I endeavor to invoke emotions through my communication by words that I've attached to people and events that are important to those connected to them. Whatever the event and whoever the individual, my purpose is to help people to feel, remember, and perhaps relive emotions and feelings from special moments, even if only for a moment.

The People They Knew is a collection of elegies, dedications, other poems, and writings that I have written over the years. I sincerely believe that people are worth remembering beyond the generation that knew them and in ways that could perhaps immortalize their memory. I also believe that the myriad of sentiments from the heart of mankind should be communicated through writing so that humanity may share and perhaps be able to articulate what is in their own hearts.

This book is a memorial for those who have loved ones whose lives are captured within its pages and for those whose accomplishments are reflected as well. *The People They Knew* is also for those who seek to find comfort, inspiration, and encouragement through literary works such as this.

In Loving Memory
of
Mr. Frank Powell, Sr.

Oh, how we stand alone and ponder
Of that soul that's gone up yonder
As we stare, our hearts grow fonder
For the one that blessed wings have borne

Echoes of our loved one parted
Safely in our minds are guarded
Songs of memories have started
They sing the one that blessed wings have borne

The tears roll down our faces so sadly
Receive him back? We'd do so gladly
Oh, how our hearts do ache so badly
For the one that blessed wings have borne

Surely, softly, sweetly, silently
Farewell whispers, exhale quietly
Left behind, we'll wait here tirelessly
To greet the one that blessed wings have borne.

Elegies

In Loving Memory

of

His Holy Grace

Bishop

Bernard Marcell Mann

Founder, Senior Pastor

and

Prelate

of

In God We Trust International Ministries

My Soul Is Thirsty No More

I was born with a thirst for the waters of sin
A craving, a panging that grew down within
At its wells and pumps, I indulged until full
To only fall sin-sick again and again
From drinking the waters of sin, of sin
The poisonous waters of sin

The poison therein did an affliction incite
My soul, my heart, they ached day and night
The life I then lived was not barren or dry
But bursts of troubled water broke dike after dike
For drinking the waters of sin, of sin
Because of the craving and panging within
I had to gulp deeply the waters of life
The bitter black waters of life

How bitter they were for their true sweetness was lost
To sip, to drink sweetness, there was a great cost
I thirsted for water no other could bring
But a Savior with passion, my thirst did accost

Alas, no more drinking the waters of sin, of sin

Slighter the craving and panging within

Bitter black waters of life now o'er frost

I now drink the blood mingled waters of the cross.

My thirst, although wetted, was not duly quenched

Not living, not thriving, but to the shores of life, I clenched

And yet the quest for water filled my thirsty soul

But no streams could be found with which my life to drench

Still, I refused the waters of sin, of sin

Fighting the craving and the panging within

I searched for the waters until my last breath

Breath drawn after sipping the chilly waters of death

And with that last breath ending, a breath is breathed anew

New life, new shores, a holy land that's filled with dew

I found no need to search for flowing waters afresh

But a holy hand extended, offered wine of deep red hue

No presence of the waters of sin, of sin

And absence of a craving and panging within

My soul is thirsty no more for waters benign

For I drink, new, with my Savior, not water but wine.

In Loving Memory

of

His Holy Grace

The Right Reverend

Bishop

Ted G. Thomas, Sr.

General Board Member

of the

Church of God in Christ, Inc.

Prelate of the Historic Virginia First Jurisdiction

"I've Just Met the Man Who Preached through Me"

Here on the brink of glory, I can hear my preaching voice

On the cusp of Beulah Land

While walking light on golden sand

The words I preached, on earth to man

Loud and clear, I hear it

It makes my heart rejoice

To hear, in heaven, a sermon

In my own preaching voice.

Here and there, I search around, still the voice I hear so pure

No words come from down within

I heed and look 'round every bend

Preaching, to man, against his sin

Loud and clear, I hear it

It's my cadence, I am sure

No doubt it is my sermon

The words I hear so pure

Here and now, a man appears, and it is the Son of God

From His lips comes the sound

I'm acquainted with how He expounds

To His words, I've always been bound

Loud and clear, I heard it

Speaking His words on earth's sod

I've just met the man who preached through me

The preaching Son of God.

In Loving Memory

of

His Holy Grace

Bishop

William Preston Wiggins, Sr.

Doctor of Divinity

Founding Pastor

of the

New Mount Joy Food For Living Ministry

Founder of the

W. P. Wiggins Bible College

Chief Apostle and Prelate

of the

United Church of God Fellowship

Journey to the Horizon

There on the horizon

I saw my journey's end

And with that insightful vision

My Christian work began

I confessed to my Lord and Savior

Tarried for the Holy Ghost

Girded up my loins with truth

And took my anointed post

I preached the Gospel from street corners

And pulpits here and there

I made the cries of Jesus Christ

Salvation I did declare

Onward as a mighty warrior

For my God's employ

I and all those sent to me

Founded House of Joy

As the days went forward

New Mount Joy became the name

And the Lord increased the fold

As Jesus was proclaimed

The horizon became closer

And the journey's road did narrow
But I knew my God was watching me
The same as He did the sparrow…

Again the message of Jesus Christ
Caused the house to be filled
And so the United Church of God
Took on the task to build
God's hand was strong upon the work
He made it to progress
I oversaw the faithful saints
And we realized sweet success
My running was so steady
I noticed not the road
So quickly and so suddenly
I had to release the load
My foot came nigh the horizon's end
But I did not want to go
And with a sweet, soft prayer, I asked
If God would take me slow
So on that glorious and fateful day
When my work's baton was passed
I began to take my last few steps
To the horizon, my eyes were cast

One last look at the world behind

Not at the work I'd done

But at my family, my wife, Lula,

My daughters and my son

To you, I leave my loving prayer

That your race will be well run

So that on that blessed day of Christ

We'll meet again on the horizon.

In Loving Memory

of

First Lady

Lula Mae Goodman Wiggins

The Stairway to Heaven

"I've Been Climbing All Along"

There I was, a blesséd newborn baby
Birthed to a world of sin and wholly dark
But in the shadows, there was a brightness shining
For Jesus came and touched my tiny heart.

I became a youthful, vibrant woman
Was not the best, but not the worst below
But in the service, God's holy Word did change me
For Jesus came and caught my falling soul.

Then for me, the title of First Lady
Mother and Wife were gifted to me too
But in mine eyes, the Savior's lowly servant
For Jesus came and made me all brand new.

After a while, my journey neared its ending
Life and work have ceased, for me, to be
Into the shadows, my soul is now returning
For Jesus came and set my spirit free.

For Jesus came and placed me on the stairway
For me, He came, and I joined the heav'nly throng
I journey onward to those gone before me
Upon the stairs I'd been climbing all along.

In Loving Memory

of

His Holy Grace

Bishop

Dwight Lee Whitfield

Founder and Chancellor

of the

PCOCH School of Ministry

Founding Pastor

of

Total Transformation House of Praise

Chief Apostle and Prelate

of the

Pentecostal Churches of Christ Holiness

Farewell from the Mountain Top

I've climbed to the top of the mountain
I scaled its slippery slopes
I had to grip each heightened cliff
And ascend without pick or rope

Treading through the paths and clefts
And places the saints once trod
My guide was the Holy Spirit
For my comfort, His staff and rod

Though treacherous a road to travel
I was able to gain much learning
God's will is only what I wanted
As I mounted, He filled that yearning

Accompanied on my upward way
God granted me grace to see
A family making the journey together
My three girls, First Lady and me

But there was a mile left to go
An occasion I could not bemoan
I had reached the peak of the mountain
And that climb was to be made alone

Life was all about this moment
My soul reaching heaven at last
I prepared to leap through the final steps
Who knew the time would come so fast?

So, I bid farewell from the mountain top
Though it hurts, I still must go
But on this side, I'll anxiously await
The day of Christ when we'll again say hello.

In Loving Memory

of

Apostle

Dallas S. Ellis, Sr.

General Overseer

United Full Gospel Revival Center

In the Meadow near the Waterfall

So quickly after the setting sun

The sun has risen aright

Though I should see the shining moon above

And feel the chill of night

No darkness dwells, only light

Because a new sun has risen aright

So quickly, after a fleeting breath

A breath is breathed once more

Though taken was the sweet and freshest air

And now a thing of yore

Celestial breeze bursts from my core

And breath is breathed once more

So quickly after the silence comes

I hear my dear Savior speak

Though dim the ears to sounds of the world

In death, they are made weak

My soul has heard His voice, unique

For my Savior, to me, does speak

So quickly after my feet leave earth

To the meadow, I am called

Though terrestrial soil and waters are gone

And my flesh beneath the pall

There remaineth a rest for me after all

Here in the meadow near the waterfall.

Pastor William E. Golden

"Where the Thankful Robins Go"

I've awakened from, what seemed, a dream
To the tune of a song I used to sing
No lyrics are heard, nor the voice of a man
But only the whistling that a robin could bring
Awakened to a brand-new day
To realize, by singing, that I've flown away
Awakened and lifted from below
Lifted to where the thankful robins go

The tune at the windowpane repeats
And as I draw closer, the bird retreats
There, onto the treetops a few feet away
I am beckoned past the garden, a man to greet
Drawn out by a tweeting little bird
To become acquainted with whom it did prefer
Drawn out, now with God in the meadow
The meadow, where the thankful robins go

The tune I heard was similar to mine
Its refrain and timing, the same design

Though the lyrics, He said, in heaven have changed
The meaning and message are along the same line
The robin was as truly grateful as you
Indeed, his singing was thanking me too
Thanksgiving brought you to the robin's window
To heaven, where the thankful robins go.

Pastor Sarah Q. Hill

One day I stood by the side of the sea

And I beheld the rising tide coming after me

The winds were great

And the land did quake

With the crashing of the waters of the sea

I turned about in search of a safe place

There was none that I could find but a rugged, old tree

No leaves were there

It stood single and bare

On the land near the waters of the sea

Protection was there lifted up from the earth

Where no water could ever come swallow me

The place was high

Forever secure was I

In the skies over the waters of the sea

Then I heard cries; someone was slipping away

I called with all my heart, "Come, be safe here at the tree."

Some ignored my plea

But others, my words received

And they were saved from the waters of the sea

Now it's been a long time since I first held on
From holding and calling, I've grown as tired as can be
The tides are high
And the slip of my foot is nigh
Nearly casting me to the waters of the sea

But in the blue yonder, I see a ship on its way
It is He who first carried and then hanged on this tree
Now with Judah, the Lion
I ride the Old Ship of Zion
On to heaven over the waters of the sea.

In Loving Memory

of

The Right Reverend

William Franklin Graham, Jr.

International Evangelist

Founder and Chairman

of the

Billy Graham Evangelistic Association

Above My Mountain

My Mountain Above

There is a place above my mountain
A dwelling place I've longed to be
Though I ne'er cast eyes upon its sands
Nor hoisted sail upon its seas

My mountain's cleft has held my peace
Its quietness, a soothing salve
A well-worn soul, this range required
Though an abode above, I'd rather have

Well-fortified was my mountainside
A family friend it came to be
But above abideth my Savior sweet
And what a friend He is to me

Upon my cliff, I breathed my last
What was mine is mine no more
Complete in thee is the hymn I sing
Now above on heaven's shores

And can it be on glorious soil
A new mountain peak for me
Above the ridge I loved below
With paradise as my scenery?

This place above my mountain abode
Was always mine; I've known
Just as I was without one plea
My Jesus received me home

Behind, on earth atop my mountain
I've left my precious loves
Of whom I pray will stand on Jesus
Till we meet on my mountain above.

In Loving Memory

of

Dr. Lois I. Evans

First Lady,

Oak Cliff Bible Fellowship

Senior Pastor,

Women's Ministries

Senior Vice President,

The Urban Alternative

Founder, Pastors' Wives Ministry

The Womb, The Way, The Wonder

A dark and troubled way to birth
And into a childhood so bright
The womb—a blesséd, laboring place
Its fruit, a gift of the Creator's grace
Guides to earth at God's own pace
The gate so dark
Delivers to life's shore
Life that gallops forthwith
To the way of death's door

A mode that's filled with ups and downs
And toilsome both day and at night
The way—a blesséd, redeeming road
Its cross, a favor and a heavy load
Through praying, the pathway flows
The journey, straight
A narrow walking chore
Walking that soon subsides
Ebbing into death's door

A wholly delightful appearing

New visions now burst on my sight

The wonder—a blesséd attraction above

Its song echoes mercy and whispers love

Assurance, I'll partake thereof

The flight, so swift

Terrestrial lands no more

To lands far and away

Rapturing past death's door.

Elder
Margie Davis Hall

From God's fountain flows a river
Within it, a gift from the great gift-giver
He offers gifts of grandeur or none at all
And our gift was Margie Davis Hall

But flowing rivers cannot cease
Else life therein will soon decrease
No sooner the waters reach here below
Back up to the Father, the streams do flow

Do not dismay o'er the ebbing water
For the great gift-giver receives His daughter
Back into the currents and off the shores of pain
The gift, once given, is received again

Into God's arms, our gift does rise
His welcome embrace precedes her prize
Our dear one, today, has answered God's call
The gift from God's river, Margie Davis Hall.

Deacon James L. Skinner, Sr.

One day I met the Lord and Christ
He sweetly spoke to me
And told of salvation paid in full
Offered to me for free

"My Master," I said, "what can I do
How can I give my all to you
What way shall I repay the debt
For my life refreshed and renewed."

"The price is great and too lofty a bill
No man can pay his own way
I've already offered the ransom expense,"
He said, "but go and serve others today."

"My Master," I said, "I can, and I will
I'll serve the well, and I'll serve the ill
The church I'll serve and those without
No station of service will go unfilled."

I aided my country; they said I served well
Though my family received my first fruits
The neighbors and saints, I gave them my best
They gave me fine honors and tributes

"My Master," I said, "I'll serve You one day
In that land, You promised far, far away
Just to kneel at Your throne, bow at Your feet
At Your edict or beckon, I'll go, or I'll stay."

He met me again at the sunset of life
And welcomed me home like a son
My burden to serve, He lifted as He said,
"Servant, take rest, no more service, well done."

Deacon Thomas Smith

Healed to Heaven

We tend to feel that ailing flesh
Is best with medicine healed
And when it fails, we often think that
The eternal fate is sealed

The chimes of grief and mourning
Sound the passing of a soul
The bereaved begin to gather 'round
The young ones and the old

Thoughts begin to flood the mind
Of laughter, joys, and gain
Only to be mixed with times
Of sadness, woes, and pain

"If only time were on our side,"
You hear the family say
"Then maybe he'd be healed complete
And with us here today."

But I admonish you, beloved
To see God's plan revealed
This, your loved one, not on earth
But to heaven, he was healed.

Missionary
Nadine Elizabeth Key

My Savior Asked Me to Sing

I would've simply sat beside the quiet water stream,

Rested in the meadow grass,

And listened to the whistling breeze

I would've tasted fresh-baked loaves

And sipped the wine of the king

But no sooner than I woke in glory,

My Savior asked me to sing

He must've heard the songs I sang,

My praises I would bring

Singing from my heart and soul,

Praying that sinners to Christ would cling

He must've gotten word somehow, perhaps on angels'

wings

But it seemed to deeply please Him, so,

When my Savior asked me to sing,

I could've sang, "Just as I am and that without one plea,"

Or that song I used to sing about His honor and His glory

I could've serenaded sweetly

"What love the Father has for me."

But I'd rather sing "How Great Thou Art."

Because my Savior asked me to sing

I would've simply sat and basked

In the warmth of His shining gleam

Healed and blessed forevermore as if it were an earthly

dream

I would've praised and worshipped

Never again to feel death's sting

But not till I've rendered this heav'nly request,

For my Savior asked me to sing.

Obituary
Missionary
Nadine Elizabeth Key

Missionary Nadine Key was a true woman of God, saved to the bone. Her life reflected the true love of God. She lived a life, as much as she could, in obedience to God by fulfilling the Great Commission. In her early years, she could be seen walking the streets, going to visit the sick, running errands for the shut-in, and praying in the homes of family, friends, church members, and loved ones. Once she was blessed with transportation, she added giving rides to that list. Many family members and saints were able to attend Sunday school, Sunday morning, and Sunday evening worship due to getting a ride with Missionary Key. She visited those who were behind bars, comforted the bereaved in their homes, and supported families during the final services of their loved ones. She was faithful in her kingdom work until she was physically unable to continue.

She was affectionately known as the "Jack Lady." Missionary Key would "roll jacks," sweet potato and apple, on several occasions and sell them to the anxiously awaiting workers and communities in the city. Her proceeds would produce finances to supplement her home and family, and often the proceeds would help to further the cause of church endeavors.

Missionary Key loved to sing the praises of her Savior. Her deep bellowing tones and sometimes soaring tunes were filled with the Spirit and anointing of God. Rarely, if ever, was she without an appropriate song of praise. Never was there a time that can be recalled where she was unwilling or unprepared to sing to the glory and honor of her God and to the content and sometimes the conviction of an awaiting audience.

She was a long-time member of New Paul's Temple Church under the leadership of Bishop Paul Armstrong and, later, Pastor Catherine Skinner. She remained until she was later called to assist in launching the ministry of Rock of Hope Church under the leadership of her brother, Elder Michael Eaton. After Rock of Hope was called to a spiritual transition, Missionary Key pledged her membership to St. Paul Baptist Church under the leadership of Bishop Clarence V. Russell III.

During her last days, Missionary Key made her way to the house of the Lord and made it her business to lift up praise to her God no matter how ill she felt. She was a supporter and a welcoming presence even in her times of illness. Her life and work will forever speak for her. She will be greatly missed.

Missionary Nadine Key is predeceased by her husband, Mr. Birven Key, her parents, Mr. James N. Eaton and Missionary Leviathan F. Eaton, and her brother, Mr. Eric Eaton. Her memory will be cherished in the hearts and minds of her two sons, Darryl Eaton (Mary), Titus Key (Widad), and three daughters, Sonya Key, Yoni Futrell (Steve), and Cassie Williams (James).

Her brothers and sisters will also hold fast to her memory. Those siblings are four brothers, Minister Gene Eaton (Joyce), Pastor Michael Eaton (Sharon), Mr. Dwight Eaton (Pam), and Mr. Rodney Eaton (Diane), and two sisters, Doris Eaton and Versa Willett.

To inherit her legacy, Missionary Key leaves a host of grandchildren, great-grandchildren, nieces, and nephews.

Missionary Ida Welch

Will the flowers ever bloom again
Now that you are gone?

Can the warmth of spring and summertime
Rejuvenate our bond?

Will this rain forever drench our lives
And mingle with our tears?

Will your memory simply wash away
And fulfill our deepest fears?

Can heaven's hosts love you any more
Than we did right here on earth

Will you wait for us at Jesus' feet
Or will we have to search?

So many questions o'er take our minds
And tomorrow will bring many more.

But for now, one thing will bring us peace—
Knowing that you'll forever be with our Lord!

Celebration of Life and Homegoing for Mother Constance "Connie" Colista Copeland

December 23rd, 2013

"I'm pressing on the upward way. New heights I'm gaining every day. Still praying as I onward bound. LORD, plant my feet on higher ground."

—Johnson Oatman, Jr.

She was known to many simply as Aunt Connie, though we were all her children in her eyes. It was only what seems like moments ago that we were enjoying her company—laughing at her jokes, listening intently as she told of the family history, and saying, "Amen!" to her fiery mini-sermons. So, it is with somewhat heavy hearts that the Rock of Hope COGIC, the family, and friends prepare to commit Mother Constance Colista Copeland's body to the ground—earth to earth, ashes to ashes, and dust to dust.

Since the inception of Rock of Hope COGIC in 2003,

which Mother Copeland helped to drive into motion, Mother Copeland has been a faithful member and a treasure of a church mother. Her presence in the services and in our lives was cherished and needed. She was our church mother. And a mother she was indeed, lovingly calling us her children.

Having played the piano/organ since the age of nine and having used her talent in many other places of worship throughout her life, Mother Copeland again offered her talent and became the organist of Rock of Hope Church. Her traditional style of playing and singing brought a spiritual awakening and a resolute sense of the presence of God. She sang and played with authentic worship unto God even up to the end of her life.

Mother
Constance Colista Copeland

Celebrating You

Though life is like a vapor
That passes with the dawn
Today it is here
Tomorrow it's gone

We should live as if it's music
That would play and play
And celebrate its song
Every single day

We realize in life
That our quickening breath is frail
So, we celebrate one
Whose soul has yet to grow stale

Your life was a gift
To us and to all
We will forever cherish it
Now that you've heard the heavenly call

We celebrate your victories
And praise God for your joys
We are thankful to be your children

Your little girls and boys

So, with happy, sincere hearts
And uplifted voices, we praise
We celebrate you, Aunt Connie
Thank God for your length of days.

Mother
Dorothy L. Franklin

You know what?

I've been saying it a long time

It had a certain rhythm

But not really any rhyme

"I'm blessed by the best and living in expectation."

It was my motto, my banner, my cause for celebration

And you know what? It was no hidden secret

What God had done for others,

That He'd give me the same treatment

I heard the good news that Jesus was saving souls

The day that I received Him,

He wrote my name on heaven's roll

And you know what?

Since then, I've had some sorrows

There were no rays of sunshine from yesterday to borrow

But I did not get discouraged

Because of what was happening to me

I simply looked to the Savior; a constant friend was He

You know what?

I've been saying it a long time

But now, since I'm in His presence,

I can leave that saying behind

Still blessed by the best, but no more expectation

I'm living my best life living in eternal jubilation.

Mr. Delano Roosevelt Franklin

"Maestro"

You could hear the music playing
Calmly swaying, gently laying
In the ears of all who'd hear
Maestro on the keys

You could hear the chords a-ringing
Joys a-bringing, gleefully swinging
Onto the hearts of all who'd hear
Maestro on the keys

When you heard those notes a-going
Melodies growing, the Spirit flowing
It felt as if your feet could hear
Maestro on the keys

Now those tunes from heaven rain
To ease our pain, send us down to memory lane
To fill our souls whenever we hear
Maestro on the keys.

Mother Rosa Goodman

Life on earth was short and busy
There was much to talk about and do
Though I'll spend in heaven an eternity
Still, my foes, no time to talk of you

I hadn't spent much time for business
Nor wasted time with pleasures, lewd
But in my life's few fleeting moments
I strived to give my God His due

My utmost goal, this side of heaven
Was to gain my mansion in the sky
I've paid my fare and signed my departure
Now I take my leave and say goodbye

I have so much to praise the Lord for
He brought me out of darkness trite
And within the twinkling of an eye
God graced me with His marvelous light

Today I stand before my Savior
The just and holy judge of all

To hear the words I've long-awaited,

"Come into the welcome hall."

Remember, dears; we'll meet at the river

If our lives are spent in godly truth

Don't forget to save time for Jesus

So He'll reserve eternity for you.

Mother
Josephine Rachel Dixon Jones

I've reached my journey's landing

What can I do but wear a smile?

My new home: it is so beautiful

I think I'll dance for a while

Just as it had on earth

The Spirit upon me falls

And I feel like running through troops

And leaping over walls

My praise is ten times greater

And my worship is fit for my king

I join the holy chorus

And with the angels, I sing

Oh, to sing before my Lord

As He welcomes me along

While He guides me o'er the skyline

To Him, I sing this song:

Wonderful Jesus, my Lord and Savior
How I love You, to me You are everything
Your promise is true; glory divine!
For You, my heart will forever sing

Now that I rest upon this golden shore
Enjoying God's promise in every way
Just one other thought thrills my soul—
That's knowing my family will join me one day.

Mother
Anna Cardell Porter

His tender hands have welcomed me

To brighter lands, that's where I'll be

My soul in flight

Doth leave the night

In God's own care, I'm safe and free

In heaven's breeze, I rest from toil

Secure from harm on celestial soil

In God's pure light

All things made right

In calm that none could ever spoil

No sickness or the pain of flesh

But health and healing righteousness

No ills to fight

Or dreadful plight

Now all I know is life refreshed

One thing remains my longing prayer

That you would climb the golden stairs

Up to these heights

With holy might

A blesséd meeting in the air.

Sister
Luvenia Yvette Callum

Has the sun on my life set already
When its rising just seemed so fresh?
Can its time of brightly shining
For all eternity be at rest?

Has the vigor of its light gone dim
When its brilliance once fiercely shone?
Can the vibrant lamp that led me
Now leave me in the dark alone?

Who can pass this cold, dark horizon
Without the sun's blazing rays?
To glimpse at its fast disappearance
Must mean the end of my days

But hark, there, a sound is blasting!
A noise of which never I heard
And behold, a sight is appearing
Forever this darkness to purge

A new sphere of my life is now starting

With my courses of earth all run

The heavens all welcome my arrival

Heaven, where Jesus is the bright, blazing sun

Today I begin my new journey

There is so much to do and see

Be sure my family and friends

To make your home in heaven with me.

Sister Ruth Golden

I now give honor to my God and to Jesus Christ, His Son

As I testify before the angels

And tell of the happiness I've won

God wraps His arms around me as He takes me by the hand

Then He leads me about the heavens

And welcomes me to Glory Land

We walk throughout my new home, and I don't worry about

pain in my knees

When God showed me my new yard

It was filled with children and pecan trees

All the children here call me Aunt Dink, and they say they

love me a bunch

I think when Easter rolls around

I'll throw them an Easter egg hunt

There's no more dragging these old feet or scuffling along

with a cane

But I'll forever sing *hallelujah*

And dance in Jesus' name

Old slew foot thought he had me, sinking in sin for sure

But from those waters, I've been lifted

Now I'm on God's peaceful shore

The love of Jesus, my Savior, has brought me here to dwell

Now to you, my family and friends

Let His love bring you here as well.

In Memorial Birthday Celebration for Sister LaVerne "LA" Johnson

July 16th, 2010

The time has come again
By the cycle of the earth
With springtime's rise and wane
Comes the celebration of my birth

Each year I've lost on earth
I've gained in heaven's time
On the shores of earth, I was fifty
In heaven, I'm only nine

Don't worry about a party
Or about singing birthday tunes
No need for cake and ice-cream
Decorations, cards, or balloons

To carry on my legacy

Would be the perfect gift for me
Hold God and each other closer
Live and love like true family

To truly celebrate my day
Live life within God's care
And when you get to heaven
I promise to greet you there.

Mrs. Marsha Forbes

My morning wings have come

And brought me to my rest

Gale winds, strongly blowing

Guide me o'er life's crest

This place I've long been seeking

Never again to be forlorn

With the light from heaven

My soul is gently warmed

My morning wings have come

And flown me to this end

And with my journey's landing

I've begun my life again

With the dew of early day

My spirit is now refreshed

All my cares have gone away

Now my every thought is blessed

My morning wings have come

And I fly from o'er earth's view

Though I must say farewell now
I will wait patiently for you.

Mrs. Margaret Ann Hardesty

My flower garden here above
Oh, what a sight to see
Of every type and color known
It's just the place for me

As far as the horizon spans
And as wide as a mountain range
This lovely spread of efflorescence
Surrounds my personal grange

I would till this blessed paradise
And be sure to keep it well
But there's a lowly gardener
My efforts he does quell

Sometimes I often think he's more
Than what he appears to be
But if he's the Savior and this is heaven
That's quite alright with me

So I'll enjoy my flower garden
And the splendid atmosphere

The Gardener and I will pass the time

Until you meet us here.

Mrs. Eloise A. Kigler

Traveling up the golden stairs
To my God's heaven, bright and fair
While I climb towards that land
My trusted Savior takes my hand

That Holy City built foursquare
Its awesome essence draws me there
Moving closer to my heavenly fate
Zion songs I hear at the gate

Now that I'm home, I shed all care
I rest in my promised mansion in the air
Reassured by God that this is my place
I recall my prayers and His saving grace

I've been given a white robe to wear
All the riches of glory are mine to share
One prayer still remains, and to it I hold,
"Lord, lead my family up the staircase of gold."

Mrs. Cathy Pope-Mosely

Sands of Time

Who fills each one's hourglass
With the sands of time?
And why does it appear today
That he did not fill up mine?

Yesterday my way was bright
The day seemed broad and long
And within the twinkling of an eye
My sands of time were gone

Can someone show me where he dwells?
To that place, I'll quickly flee
The question burns within my soul,
"Did he intend on slighting me?"

There's so much left behind to do
For my babies and home need care
These things he may not understand
I must make him aware

Though my sands of time have slipped away
And shortened my life below
There is one thing left that should be said
And this to you I'll now bestow

My sands of time on earth were few
And that is known with certainty
But now that I've transcended time
My sands above will last for eternity.

Mrs. Benette Puller

If Souls Could Sing…

If our souls could sing the songs of the heart
They'd resound the lyrics that only the lips could part

We'd sing of the joys and sorrows we shared
And bellow in laughter at the things we dared

The medley of our cries and hurts would ring
To remind us of the comfort to each other we'd bring

In perfect voice, our souls would blend
The earthly sounds to completely transcend

Whispers of love, our hearts would bring
Songs to last forever—if only our souls could sing.

Ms. Janelle Boyette

Some people came and enhanced our lives
Some blew away like debris
But whatever the weather, we've stayed together
Us three
Mom, DeeDee, and me

There was once just one, my mother, Ms. B.
But God twice grew the family tree
And from that day to this, we've grown as one
Us three
Mom, DeeDee, and me

So, why should this change and be broken up?
Shall death break our bond free?
No, we'll meet again someday o'er the crystal sea
Us three
Mom, DeeDee, and me

I'll ever be with you, living in your hearts
Just take a look within, and you'll see
No matter what comes, it will always be
Us three
Mom, DeeDee, and me.

Ms. Tiffany Bynum

He Calmed My Raging "C"

I would have never thought
That someday I would be
Suddenly overtaken by a raging C
Observing my life's waters
Flowing full and free
They never showed the slightest threat
Of ever drowning me

Then rapid waves came splashing
Their crash was like a dream
Relentlessly came rushing, angrily it seemed
Taking health and all my strength
Left suffering the sting
Till I could hardly bear the brunt
Of the C's furious lashing

Somehow a thought began
And my mind and soul decreed
There is a God whose voice commands the raging C
Wind and waves obey His will

He speaks the peace to be
The C obeys; my soul is loosed
Its raging, now, does cease.

Ms. Carolyn B. Garland

Now that I've gone on to glory
I'd like to share my journey's story
How sweet the way though rough and hilly
My roads were lined with the calla lily

How white the lily on my life's road
My Savior and His presence—my soul's abode
The Holy Spirit to light my path
And to take me up when I've breathed my last

How yellow the lily on my life's road
My family and friends, helping to bear my load
In times of health and in times of pain
In sunshiny days and in seasons of rain

How pink the lily on my life's road
My only daughter in whom my love was sewn
Her heart was mine, and mine was in her hands
Our lives held together with unbreakable bands

Though on this day our flesh cannot meet
We can meet again soon at the Savior's feet

In spite of my test and whatever my mode
I'm glad that I chose the calla lily road.

Ms. Rena Scarbrough

Nevermore the desert sands

With nothing there to glean

Nor the sting of cactus plants

But only fields of green

Nevermore the drowning seas

With darkness in the deep

Nor the waves that conquer all

But only fields to reap

O, the winds of heaven's sky

The joyful atmosphere

'Twas my God that drew me nigh

His love has brought me here

Nevermore, the valley low

With lonely walls, so steep

Nor the endless, rocky road

But only fields that greet

Nevermore the miry marsh

With sludge so hard to dredge

Nor the muddy, swampy muck
But only fields of sedge

Now goodbye to earthly time
Adieu 'til we convene
You be sure to claim your prize
Eternity in fields of green.

Mr. Kenneth R. Armstrong, Sr.

Well, I've finally gone up yonder
To go the way of countless others
And there awaiting my entrance
Are my father and my mother

A greater joy surrounds me
Since I've reached this tableland
Uncle Paul extends heaven's fellowship
With the shaking of my right hand

Well, I've finally gone up yonder
For those who are concerned
And no sooner my feet strike Zion
I'm eating crab legs with LaVerne

I meet the saints who've gone before
They all greet me back in love
And finally, my Savior meets me
With a pair of golden boxing gloves

Well, I've finally gone up yonder
Though a bit earlier than I would've thought
But this is the place that I've longed for
This, the paradise that I sought

Come, wife and sons and daughters
Brothers and sisters, please don't wander
Loved ones and friends, make preparations
To finally come up yonder.

Mr. Eric Eaton

With my helmet tucked underneath my arm
I stuck my sword in the golden sand
I breathed what seemed celestial air
And began to tread the tableland

In the distance, I saw a woman
It was my mother, who instantly smiled
Then, she cried out in happiness,
"Lord, have mercy; here comes my child!"

I embraced my mother and kissed her
Then, with my dear mother, I talked
I pondered questions as we wandered
She listened intently as we walked

She told me to take the hand of a man
Who was sitting far away
That man separates the right from the wrong
My time for separation was today

He offered to take my breastplate,
My shoes, and my shield of faith

He proceeded to lead my dear mother and I
Through the throne room's gate

I immediately realized then and there
That I had stumbled on heaven's greeting
And that Jesus had led me to the place
Where there was about to be a meeting.

Mr. John Groves

Heavenly Groves

Today I walk in new, crisp air
And the presence of the Lord is with me there
Along a quaint and a quiet road
He walks with me through heavenly groves

He lifts and cheers my once ill soul
And speaks of great wonders on our stroll
We taste of wine and freshly baked loaves
While He walks with me through heavenly groves

No danger seems to come our way
Ne'er comes the night; it remains the day
Winter is no more; no need for a stove
We walk in His warmth through heavenly groves

I do not seek for our journey's end
For I reap grand splendors 'round ev'ry bend
I only await those from my earthly abode
To come walk with Him and me through heavenly groves.

Mr. Stanley Tarkenton, Sr.

Where is it that you've gone?

Can you return to say?

From these words do not diverge

Tell your direction's way

Can I soon follow on

From land to journey's flight?

Tell of new birth, goodbye to earth

Where is that runway's light?

From the valley to the skies

Tell me how to set my pace

Where do I turn? Must I discern?

Can I be told its place?

Tell of the splendors there

Where life is good and fair

Can all be heard within your words?

From yonder hear my prayer

Where is it that you've gone?

Can you speak of your abode?

From this, your dear, I hope you hear
Tell me how you found that road.

Mr. Jermal G. Williams

Unforgettable spaces

Look-a-like faces

Traces of you in familiar places

Your voice heard in breezes

This, my sorrow, eases

Your love remains, and my heart it pleases

You slipped through my grasp

To eternity you've passed

Within my heart, forever you'll last

Each day I'll keep praying

And asking God, saying,

"Lord, keep his memory from fraying."

Alas, now you sleep

And for this loss, I do weep

For the burden of sadness, comfort I seek

But with time, I'll get better

God will break sorrow's fetter

And turn this great storm into fair weather.

Mr. Ben J. Willett, Sr.

My Wife and Friend

I felt your love, and it moved me so
But I could not understand
How such an overwhelming passion
Could be lavished upon one man

I've loved and lost time and time again
How the world can be so cruel
Never imagined I'd find the souls
Truly living the golden rule

But, oh, what a friend I found in you
And in your children as well
Respect and loyalty showing
My own love and devotion compelled

I may have seemed a little bit cold
At all being given at will
I did not know just how to react
So, I gave things, and I paid the bills

But all is not lost nor left for naught
Love, it endured till the end
Though I've now slipped away in death
You're still my wife and my friend.

The Newtown, Connecticut, Victims

December 14th, 2012

In flight beyond the skies
I feel the wind surround me
Oh, the sights before my eyes
They make my heart so free

No remembrance of the pain
My mind knows only glory
And my lips sing a refrain
Of a new and happy story

Don't mourn so very long
Know I am ever with you
Family, please be strong
I'll never bid you adieu

Don't fear; though hard it seems
I'll be there in your memory
You'll see me in your dreams
To comfort you so gently

Now live on by heaven's grace
Soon your days will get bright
Until then, be filled with faith
Till we meet again in flight.

In Loving Memory

of

The Emanuel Church Nine

Rev. Clementa Pinckney

Rev. Daniel Simmons, Sr.

Rev. DePayne Middleton Doctor

Rev. Sharonda Coleman-Singleton

Cynthia Hurd

Ethel Lance

Myra Thompson

Susie Jackson

Tywanza Sanders

The Emanuel Church Nine

The hallowed aisles and lifted places
Stained glass windows and tufted kneeling spaces
The dignity of a house of worship, refined
Now absent from its grandeur, the Emanuel Church Nine

They knew not of that dreadful rival
That sat amongst them as they studied the Bible
The weapons of that strongman, they were unable to bind
And into that good night went the Emanuel Church Nine

There, in the holiest of God's heavenly domain
Is a place prepared for such departed souls to remain
There, no more a strongman will they find
But eternally with Jesus; He and the Emanuel Church
Nine.

Eulogy

In Loving Memory
of
Ms. Viola M. Hines

"Come unto me, all ye that labour and are heavy laden, and I will give you rest. Take my yoke upon you, and learn of me; for I am meek and lowly in heart: and ye shall find rest unto your souls. For my yoke is easy, and my burden is light" (Matthew 11:28–30).

In this scripture, the words of Jesus are intended to bring comfort to the hearers in His day and the readers of today. He says that if you are carrying a burden or a heavy weight, go to Him, and He will give you rest from it. But at the same time that He extends rest from a burden, He also extends the invitation to what seems to be another burden. He says to take His yoke on you. However, the correct interpretation of this scripture suggests that the yoke of Jesus is not a burdensome yoke. In fact, He says that it is easy and that His burden is light. It is, nevertheless, a yoke. Yet, He implies that, though you will experience some burden and labor, He will be under the load with you and make it manageable for you to bear it.

Anybody who knew Ms. Hines and was acquainted with her via Facebook knew that she was very interactive on that platform. Post a picture, an obituary, a funny meme, a heartfelt message, or a thought-provoking quote, and Ms. Hines was sure to give a response. But it wasn't just any response. Ms. Hines seemed to put her everything into her responses. She seemed to choose her words and emojis with great intent. Ms. Hines didn't just respond, but she almost took the occasion on as if it were her own. She shared it with you. In happy times, she was genuinely happy with and for you. In times of celebration, you couldn't keep her from posting emojis. It was her celebration too. In times of sadness and grief, Ms. Hines not only made sure that the obituary notice was without error but, with her deepest and warmest words, she would, in the same manner as our Lord Jesus, come under the yoke of your burden with you to help make it manageable for you to bear it.

We would do well to follow in the footsteps of our Lord and Savior Jesus Christ and to follow the example of Ms. Hines—to take on a spirit of meekness and lowliness of heart for one another, to genuinely celebrate with others, to take on the sorrows of others as our own, and help them to bear them. Ms. Hines did this for others, and today Christ has done it eternally for her. Jesus has forever taken her burden, relieved her of her labor, and given her rest for her soul.

May the Lord Jesus bring the comfort that only He can to those left here to celebrate her memory.

—Humbly Submitted,

Dr. & Mrs. Calvin & Tabitha Franklin

And family

Eulogy

In Loving Memory

of

Mr. Birven Key

Loving from a Broken Place

"Beloved, let us love one another: for love is of God; and everyone that loveth is born of God, and knoweth God. Beloved, if God so loved us, we ought also to love one another" (1 John 4:7, 11).

To truly love the type of people who live in this world, you must first master the virtue of mercy. There's an adage that says, "Mercy understands the why behind the what." That understanding helps put life in a very humbling perspective. The need for mercy in the event of our own failures often places us in a different point of view when it comes to the failures of others. It isn't until you truly understand people through the eyes of mercy that you can love them as you truly ought.

Speaking of love, our Lord and Savior, Jesus Christ, though sinless and perfect, was born into a broken world. For example, His people were under the harsh oppression and rule of the Roman Empire. Though His parents were royal descendants of King David, the regard that He should have received as royalty was non-existent. Very early on in His life, this broken world began to break Him. He was born into a broken world, and He lived in a broken world. John 1:11 says, "He came unto His own, and His own received Him not." Eventually, that broken world did to Him what it seems to do to everyone—it crucified Him. The amazing thing is that out of all that, Christ still loved the world from the broken place of a cruel cross. *(While we were yet sinners, Christ died for us...)* Uncle Birven's story is not much unlike that of Jesus. Though, in the same manner as us all, Uncle Birven's story is peppered with the effects of sinful flesh.

Into a Broken Place, He Was Born

The Scripture says in Romans 5:12 that sin came into the world through one man—Adam. Scripture also states that we are all born in sin. Uncle Birven was not excluded. Add to that the brokenness that sprang forth in and from his own life. He endured family hardships growing up, some of which are beyond what some of us could even comprehend. Life was not his best friend at times. I don't have to go into any details. Just think of your own life experiences and how those times may have taken a toll on you from a very early age. He was born into a broken place, and yet he still grew up to be a man of character. He didn't let brokenness destroy everything about him. On top of that, he was a Black man living in America. Take that home and ponder it for a while! Still, he married a wife; together, they brought sons and daughters into the world, and he worked to take care of his family. He provided a home—a place where his wife, those sons, and daughters could live and thrive. And with that, he started another road in his life's journey. However, he had to walk that journey from a broken place. Almost like Jesus—born into a broken world, then He gathered His disciples and began His journey from a broken place.

From a Broken Place He Lived

As Jesus journeyed, many of the people could not understand who Jesus was and why He was doing the things that He did. They could not make sense of why He said the things that He said. On the other hand, some did not want to understand. In like manner, Uncle Birven endured hurts inflicted on him, but he kept it moving. He experienced those who could not understand the person that he had become and why. Some refused to understand, and others turned away forever because of it. Perhaps, it was because of the hurts that Uncle Birven may have inflicted on others. *(This may be the one difference between Uncle Birven's story and that of Jesus, as it relates to loving from a broken place.)* Uncle Birven had to deal with those mistakes. We all make mistakes for which we must endure regrets and remorse. Sometimes these hurts never seem to go away no matter what we do. And again, the people who could possibly help have gone away. But even with that weight on his shoulders, Uncle Birven loved deeply.

From a Broke Place He Loved

The saying goes, "Hurt people hurt people." Though that is a true statement, when we look at Jesus, who was hurting in a tremendous way while on the cross, He did not make that statement true. As He hung dying, His words were those of forgiveness—a thing which would help those crucifying Him and was most certainly from a place of love. Uncle Birven pressed through his brokenness, and no matter how much he fussed, he always asked about the well-being of his family. He would always ask how we were moving toward success. He never failed to inquire about our plans for the future. He loved us deeply, even from a broken place. I believe that he understood and practiced, the best that he could, the virtue of mercy. Because he needed it, he knew that others did as well, which is why he loved so deeply.

My cousin Cassie, Uncle Birven's daughter, and I were hired for a job at a company quite a distance from our home. She and I had no way to get back and forth to that job, but we took it anyway. When he heard that we were trying to make moves toward success, he got an old car and tinkered with it until it started. Mind you, the car barely got up to fifty miles per hour, but it served its purpose. The point is that Uncle Birven wasn't a rich man. He gave us what he could from a place of love.

When I visited Uncle Birven to announce my intent to get married, he had both "guns" loaded, ready to fuss me out. He wasn't upset at the fact that I was getting married. However, when I told him that "I had to get married," he was concerned that I felt the need to marry, perhaps, because I had impregnated a young lady ahead of time instead of doing things the right way and settling down first with someone with which I could continue to build a life. That wasn't the case. In fact, things were done correctly. I just wanted to get married, and I told him as much. Uncle Birven was visibly relieved, and he put his "guns" away. Again, his concern was from the root of his love for me. Closer to the end of his life, he left a bit of marital advice for me from a place of brokenness. Not only was he sick, but his own marriage, for reasons known to him and my aunt, had ended several years before. However, he loved me enough to advise me, "Put your trust completely in God alone. If you both trust in God completely, you'll be able to do right by each other."

I simply believe that memories will serve us better if we look at them through the lens of mercy. Jesus loved us from a broken place. And though He did not deserve the cruelty inflicted upon Him, He still looked on mankind with mercy and loved us deeply. Uncle Birven also loved us from a broken place, and because of that brokenness and his own need for mercy, I believe that he was able to extend mercy to others and love them deeply as well. We ought to follow their examples and look through the lens of mercy, understand the why behind the what, and love one another even if it's while they are in a broken place or if it's from a broken place of our own.

Dedications

Mr. Nelson Rolihlahla Mandela

I Am South Africa

I am flesh, and I am blood
My name gives them royalty
Forever mingled within its majesty
I am South Africa, and South Africa is me

Named through dynasty and renamed of men
My rights give them new degree
Now tuned within its chants and songs
I am South Africa, and South Africa is me

I've hoped to live, and I've lived prepared to die
The ideal—self-governing society
Filled with its voices of harmony
I am South Africa, and South Africa is me

Out of apartheid and into accord
Our prize—democratic presidency
An estranged son, now with my nation reconciled
I am South Africa, and South Africa is me.

Mr. Barack Obama

Gift of a Son

Over a rushing sea of bitterness
A son has settled a home
Thrusting free from humble beginnings
He made that land his throne

Not wielding vile fits of power
To gain grandeur of tower and steeple
But the heart of this son is to honor
And to be a defender of the people

Who compares to the great giver of gifts?
Who? Who is like God?
How blessed we are to receive this gift
That leads by instruction and rod

The rays of the future were slightly bent
Now its days are no longer bleak
The rushing, bitter seas once traveled
By this son are now made sweet.

Barack   *Blessed*

Michelle   *Who is like God?*

Sasha   *Defender of the People*

Malia   *Sea of Bitterness*

Obama   *Slightly Bent*

Her Majesty Queen Elizabeth II

By the grace of God,

Of The

United Kingdom and Great Britain

And

Northern Ireland

And of

Her other realms and territories Queen,

Head of the Commonwealth,

Defender of the faith.

God and My Right

A Birthday Dedication

The royal right

God's finished fight

Its foes, defeated with His own pure light

And with victory's rest

He endowed and blessed

The Queen

Through Windsor blood aright

The royal crown

God's own renown

On heads of kings, it is let down

And from the Abbey

Came forth majesty

Hail, The Queen

From Windsor, lown

The royal throne

It is His own

On which He seated flesh, blood, and bones

And from His seat

The nation did greet

Queen Elizabeth

Of the Windsor home

The royal role

God's pen and scroll

The names of kingdoms, young and old

And from His quill

The ink does spill

As He writes of

The Windsor household.

Dr. Maya Angelou
A Memorial Dedication

Written

to

Ms. Oprah Winfrey

Now that my sweet mother is gone

Who's gonna lead me?

The phenomenal dancer, writer, and singer of songs

The one-of-a-kind inspiration of a lifetime

Now lifted from earth into the heavenly throng

Now that she's gone

Who's gonna lead me?

Now that my sweet mother is gone

Who's gonna lead me?

The teacher, the preacher,

The chastiser who's wiser

The insightful intellect, O, the intuition

My first lady elect

Now risen to reap of heaven's best

So, who's gonna lead me?

Now that my sweet mother is gone

Who's gonna lead me?

Her presence gone from this side of glory's shore

Of heritage, descendant, now progenitor

A vault of life's real answers

To her dear child, a mentor

Though she'll not lead me as before

With words of new life's rhythm

And a voice out from heaven's door

By wings of angels borne

Mother will still lead me.

LaShun Pace

Heaven is My Goal

It's in my clapping; it's in my stomping
It's in the waving of my hands
Through my singing, praises ringing
Through the way I do my dance
As I tread up, I hold my head up
There's a holy sway in my stroll
I'm paving my way as I go

After all, heaven is my goal

Ever helping, ever reaching
Ever giving my all in all
To tell His story, offer glory
Surrendering my life whatever befall
As I go through, I give God His due
There springs up reverence from my soul
I'm paving my way as I go

After all, heaven is my goal

Through some crying, through some hurting
Through time of total fret

I keep on pressing, seldom resting
Never afraid to break a sweat
As I run on, I look for glory's dawn
And I wait to hear yonder's roll
I'm paving my way as I go
After all, heaven is my goal.

Ms. Robin René Roberts

An Inspirational Dedication

Did pain incite a darkened cry
Or hurt invite a groan?
Did thoughts of knowing life beyond
Bemoan the earthly home?

Did life seem short when ills prevailed
Or long when treatments failed?
Did tides of wonder wax and wane
And make your faith grow frail?

Did fate bewail your victory
Or your healing from above?
Did hands contrary to your will
Conflict with hands of love?

If, for you, all these rang true
You made it hard to know!
In spite of ev'ry challenge seen
Your smile did overflow!

Because of all your going through
Some may have felt despair
But when I saw your golden gleam
It moved me into prayer

I had to write a word to you
A poem sent to inspire
Because of how you journeyed on
Through paths that were bemired

I pray that strength will dwell with you
In the days and years ahead
And that God's favor covers you
Whatever paths you tread.

Mrs. Versa M. Willett

A Christmas Dedication

Divinely Chosen Roses

Amid one Christmas years ago
A rose did carry seed
And weeks before that holy day
Her labor did proceed

Then on a Sunday afternoon
The little bud did bloom
The voice of God had called him forth
A blessing from the womb

Twice more, the voice spoke to the womb
And called rose four and five
Divinely gardening all the lives
And making them to thrive

Five in all made up that bunch
Called in the yesteryear
Each time the Gardener spoke a word
The roses did appear

As we approach this Christmas Day
We're thankful to our Lord
For what a gracious rose He gave
Mother, uniquely our reward

Unlike the blossoms in a store
With ribbons and lace emboldened
This bouquet of lively roses
Was divinely chosen.

A Special Presentation

in Appreciation

to

Dr. Jasper Saunders

&

Dr. Janice Saunders

President and Vice President

of the

W. P. Wiggins Bible College

Suffolk, VA

For centuries, the ring, outside of being worn as simple jewelry, has represented at least three major human attributes—commitment, achievement, and authority. The ring of commitment, better known as the wedding band, is an endless circle, with no beginning and no end, representing the sentiments of the marriage vow. The ring of achievement is worn as a token of success, representing the hard work put into gaining victory. Rings of that sort are the championship ring and the class ring. But the ring of authority is unique as it can be readily employed to convey the sentiments of the wearer, be he the owner or the messenger of the owner. It is a stamp or a seal of power, and it expresses truth and authenticity. This ring is the signet ring.

Nowadays, society has all but done away with the ring of commitment and all that it has represented throughout the ages. The ring of achievement has seemingly become more valuable and appealing to the eye than the education and the work that goes into obtaining that which is only a symbol. And the signet ring seems to no longer be given as a symbol of a revered station of authority but given to whoever covets the ring and has the façade of the worth and ability to wear it. However, today, this fifth day of June in the year of our Lord 2021, we, the Doctoral Class of the W. P. Wiggins Bible College, in appreciation to Dr. Jasper Saunders, President, and Dr. Janice Saunders, Vice President—two individuals who stand out in the community of faith and education as giants in both arenas—presents keepsake signet rings and a certificate as tokens of our gratitude and eternal appreciation for their immense fervor and persistence to educate people of faith in the faith.

—The W. P. Wiggins Bible College Doctoral Class of 2021

A Parable in Celebration
of the
Ministerial Licensing
of
Minister in Training
Tabitha M. Franklin

"The work you've done has spoken for you time and time again. But God knows best when it's time to leap into your calling."

—*Elder Dr. Calvin Franklin*

All in God's Timing

There was a master climber who was teaching a novice how to climb. They were trying to get to the highest peak of a particular mountain. And after climbing for a while, they came to a ledge that overlooked a rift in the mountainside. In order to continue climbing to get to the top of the peak, they had to jump across the rift to get to the other side. The master climber had always told the novice that timing was important when climbing the mountain. So, there they were on this ledge above the rift. There was just enough room on the ledge for the novice to get a running start to try to jump across. So, he looked up at the master climber and asked, "Is it time yet?" The master climber shook his head and said, "No, not yet." They continued walking, and the ledge started to become narrower. Now, there was not enough space for the novice to get a running start, but he thought to himself that there was still enough space to jump and make it across. So, again, he looked up to the master climber and asked, "Is it time yet?" The master climber, again, shook his head and said, "No, not yet." They kept on walking, and as they walked, the ledge became narrower and narrower. It became so narrow that they began to hug the side of the mountain to keep from falling into the gaping rift. And with fear in his eyes, the novice looked up at the master climber and asked, "Is it time yet?" The master climber responded, "Now it's time!" The novice turned, bent his knees, and leaped as hard as he could off the ledge and over the rift. He made it! The master climber followed. Once they were united on the other side of the rift, the novice asked the master climber, "Why couldn't we jump the first time? Why couldn't we jump the second time? Why did it take all the way to the last for me to be able to jump?" The master climber responded, "At the beginning, there was deep water at the bottom of the rift, and the rift was too wide. Even with a running start, you would not have made it across. You would have drowned. At the second stop, there were stones, sharp rocks, and boulders at the bottom of the rift, and the rift was too wide. You would not have been able to make it across. You would have jumped to your death. It was only there at the very end of the ledge that the conditions were exactly right for you to make it across. I know the mountain better than you, and because you trusted and waited on me, you made it across safely to continue climbing up to the mountain top."

A Parable in Celebration of the Ministerial Licensing of Minister in Training Shamika S. Dirtion

"You've been doing the work; now it's time to announce to the world whom God has called you to be."

—*Elder Dr. Calvin Franklin*

Flying in the Day

There was a mother eagle, and she was nestling her eaglets in her nest. While warming her eaglets, she began thinking about the near future and that very soon, she would have to teach them how to fly. The next day, she awoke and told them, "One day, you will have to fly like me." And with that said, she leaped from the edge of her nest and swooped down through the trees and back up into the air. She flew through the clouds, back down through the treetops, and landed back in the nest. In the weeks following, the mother eagle taught her eaglets what to do. She showed them over and over how to put what she taught them into practice. But she had yet to see them fly. After one last lesson, she told them plainly, "Tomorrow is the day that you're going to have to fly. I'm going to have to push you out of the nest, and you will have to fly." That night, they all went to sleep. But in the middle of the night, the mother eagle heard a rustling in the nest. She awoke to see her eaglets jumping off the edge of the nest, flying just slightly through the air, and landing gently back into the nest. They were already flying! When they landed once more, she asked them, "What are you doing? What's going on?" They responded, "You taught us how to fly, and we've been flying at night." In her excitement, the mother eagle said, "All we have to do now is prepare for you to start flying in the day."

A Parable
in Celebration
of the
Ordination
of
Minister
Twianna H. Darden

"You've grown into the calling on your life. While you were growing, God grew His gifts in you."

—*Elder Dr. Calvin Franklin*

Grow Into It and Let It Grow Into You

There was a young boy who sang in a community choir. He loved to sing, and he could sing very well. Everyone thought that his voice was very beautiful. But he was a young boy, and his voice did not have a very wide range. One day the choirmaster called a rehearsal. At that rehearsal, he gave the bass solo to an older boy. The older boy sang the bass part masterfully. He had a stunning voice, and he sang very well—low and deep. The young boy looked up and said to the choirmaster, "I want to sing the bass solo. That's what I'm supposed to do. I'm supposed to sing the bass solo." The choirmaster responded, "You can't do it right now. Your voice is too high. It's not going to go that low. But take this sheet music and learn it. Learn to read the music and learn the lyrics. Maybe one day, you'll get to sing the bass solo." The young boy took the sheets, and over time, he learned to read the music. Year after year, he wasn't able to sing low enough to do the solo. His voice just wouldn't get that low.

After a few years, the choirmaster called a rehearsal as

he often did. This time, the choirmaster called on the young boy and asked him to sing the bass solo. The young boy got up and began to sing. His voice was still too high. But to his surprise, and all of a sudden, it cracked and went very low. The young boy began singing in a beautiful, deep, and low bass tone. After the song was done, the choirmaster said to the young boy, "You did well. You learned the music and the lyrics, and your voice came when it should. You grew into the part, and the part grew into you." From then on, he was no longer the young boy but the bass soloist.

Other Poems

Poems of Passion

Crying Sky

Oh, crying skies, tell me once again
Why can't the love I sought be mine?
Speak, weeping clouds of gray
Utter the answer and, to my question, be kind

Why, oh crying skies, are you silent?
My heart rips at each hollow beat
Speak, horrid and sunless void
Give answer to me, I beg at thy mercy seat

Tell me, in what wrong did I partake?
Was it so that my love can't be filled?
Oh, crying skies, my tears join with thine
Will my love, which sought hers, be sealed?

Picture Show

Picture show, behind my eyes

Thoughts of fantasy in disguise

Smiling faces become lies

Truth? Pictures behind my eyes

Glossy, gleaming, glittering hypocrisy

Mounds of flesh concealing photography

Liars projecting hints of monogamy

Truth? Pictures behind my eyes

Hints of falsehood and looks of guilt

Wells of fraud that lusts have built

Covering the imagined like a winter's quilt

Truth? Pictures behind my eyes

I see the one that lay beneath me

Portraits of others I view secretly

My climax? Secret portraits were the key

Truth? Pictures behind my eyes

Picture show, behind my eyes
A cancer that brings my demise
I'll let it go if I am wise!
Truth? Pictures behind my eyes.

The Majestic

The majestic appearance of an angel had come
With her, she bought laughter and love
The angel, beautiful like the rising sun

She was sent to me from above

Like none other, she cared for my heart
For my hurting, she had the cure
Her voice was an ointment for all my wounds

She is precious to me and pure

Yet now the majestic is no longer mine
Her face no longer to behold
A mortal now sealed with one that is heavenly

Her purity, soiled by my soul.

Sin Cost Me Love

Drippings of honey drops fell from my lips
Its sweetness in her ear made her mine
My feelings sailed faster than sailing ships
To be her lover was my great design

With my words, she could feel every embrace
And my voice tickled down her spine
We hungered for greetings, face to face
Though we settled for glimpses in the mind

Daily I spoke to express how I felt
Whether by phone or online
Using expressions that made her melt
Because I knew she was worth my time

The day we met, we lost ourselves in love
Our deeds flooded over like the tide
We had broken God's law written above
I had done wrong; I could not stand in pride

With all sorrow in my heart, I had to apologize
I was ashamed but had to let it all subside

My sin against God was right before His eyes
I admitted my wrong, and there, in sadness, cried

Drippings of honey drops fell from my lips
Its sweetness in her ear made her mine
Now, this love, from my grasp, has been ripped
Those glimpses are forever left behind.

Why Yet Do I Die?

Treacherous rage and beastly hate
Torment and sorrows constantly rise
Hideous and monstrous anger bursts
Gut-wrenching cries never subside

Hollow and empty, yet full of want
Desires flare hotter than the sun
Breaking of bones and gnashing of teeth
Will this fire of hell anon be done?

If my actions were right, why yet do I die?
Heart and head slowly splitting asunder
Lips so close to curse my day of birth
Dare not I, never shall my soul be plunder

So right, I die and wrong the same
Turning left, then right, and then left again
Still, I die, no matter the choice
So, I shall have my spoils along with disdain.

A Season Without the Stars

Summer brings heat and bumblebees,

Full flowing streams

And fully blossomed trees

And on a hot summer's night

One can see them from afar

A glittering, glamorous, galactic sight in the heavens

A dark sky full of stars

Autumn brings breeze and colored leaves,

Pumpkin patches

And harvest festivities

And when the day has turned dark

One can see them from afar

A billion balls of brightness burning in the heavens

A dark sky full of stars

Winter brings snow and an icy freeze,

Trips to mountain cabins

And challenging slopes with skis

And during the silent white evenings

One can see them from afar

A showing of shimmering and shining in the heavens

A dark sky full of stars.

Spring brings life and the girls that wear capris

Playground time for children

And time for elegant, outdoor teas

And when our side of the world is sleeping

One can see them from afar

A springtime spectacular spectacle displayed in the

heavens

A dark sky full of stars

Infatuation brings flutters and thoughts of bliss and ease

Bursts of whimsical fantasy

And moments of lust to seize

But when the course of time is complete

One can only see her from afar

A lonely, lauded lady, unattainable as if in the heavens

A truly dark day without the stars.

Poems for Her

Spring Flower

She is the most beautiful flower
Grown from a perfect seed
Derived from God's power
But she sees herself as a weed

She is a blossom of the spring
Worth the wait through winter's cold
The sun smiles brightly on her
To make her subtle features bold

Though she is a wonder of sight
She is blind to that fact
A reflection of God's light
Of nothing good does she lack

Wonderfully crafted indeed
Above the rest, she towers
She is not a wretched weed
But the most beautiful of flowers.

To Prove

What can I do to show that you're good enough?
What words do I say to show it's the truth?
How can I tell you about your worth?
What will make you believe it's true?

How deep must I dig to get the answer?
How much love will it take to prove?
What measures do I have to take?
How many mountains do I have to move?

Why don't you believe you are beautiful?
Why don't you believe you're good?
When will you take me at my word?
Why are my compliments misunderstood?

When will you break free from the shell?
When will you come to see the light?
Why do you challenge my faith in you?
When will you recognize that you're alright?

Where did the notion come from?

Where in your heart does it rest?

Who said that you were least of all?

Where are your thoughts of being the best?

Who came and made this happen?

Who filled your mind with lies?

Where can I dispose of this deceit?

Who is responsible for your cries?

Even though you don't believe me

Even though you think I'm wrong

I'll continue proclaiming the truth

Even though you've known it all along

I'll tell you over and over

I'll whisper so soft and dear

Even when you firmly contest me

I'll rebuttal without fear.

Free to Love Again

Lift up your heart, my child

Be not ashamed

Let your spirit free, my child

You are not to blame

Love was your lot, my dear

And it came to you

But he was not for you, my dear

His love was not true

Yes, you were laden, beloved

And filled with guilt

But on your guilt, beloved

Was your prison built

Be free from bondage, sweet dove

And fly like the wind

Live and love again, sweet dove

Let freedom your heart mend.

As the Queens

As the queens of ancient times
She stands as gracefully poised
Her golden skin gleams in radiance
Such beauty I could never avoid

Her head is fully graced
With long black strands of hair
Eyes like those of a temptress
Lips full, smooth, and fair

Shoulders of enticing width
They accent her slender neck
Ornate breasts of great lush
Strong arms that reach and beck

A belly of tender image
Her navel, kissable and sweet
Hips of incredible thickness and tone
Anatomically flowing like a steady beat

Wondrous thighs, firm and full
They glide smoothly side-by-side

She walks congenially with precious legs

With soft feet, she moves in perfect stride

As the queens of ancient times

She is sought by many eyes

She is indeed of magnificent splendor

And like the queens, her beauty will never die.

God Made Her

In the darkness, soft whispers could be heard

The angels fluttered about Him in delight

To His creatures, the craftsman revealed His plan

And He bid them to take their flight

He sat in the darkness alone with His thoughts

His heart pondered the creation to be

"How should I craft her?" He asked Himself

"And make her a reflection of Me?"

And soon, with thoughts passed, He reached to the earth

And gathered a hand full of clay

He knew in His heart that a being of such grandeur

Would cause Him to work all day

In sweat and in tears, He smoothed every curve

He fearfully molded each part

Each lock of black hair was carefully placed

To complete His great work of art

Now with a sweet, tender kiss from her maker above

Breathed a celestial soul

He called her name, and she opened her eyes

He proclaimed what a beauty to behold.

She Is the Temple
of the Lord

I dare not look at her the wrong way

Nor cross her path with unkind words to say

For such a woman as she is worthy of much more

Because this woman is the temple of the Lord

God has shaped and sculpted her and given her bright

skin

Molded for her a soft heart to make it easy for love to set

in

How effortless it is such a woman to adore

Because this woman is the temple of the Lord

And what a voice God has given her with which to sing

To lift it high in song so that comfort it can bring

When she sings God's Holy Spirit, He outpours

Because this woman is the temple of the Lord

Nothing can change who she is, not even the past

In God's eye, she is pure and worthy of her holy task

This ministry is hers; she has but to walk right through

the door

Because this woman is the temple of the Lord

Can anyone be likened to this woman of God?
Would any foot dare walk where God will cause her feet

to

Trod?

At the final day in heaven, her spirit will soar
Because this woman is the temple of the Lord.

My Earthly Everything

If there are jewels to be unearthed

And treasures yet to discover

I want no other valued thing

I'd rather have my love, my friend, my earthly everything

My jewel I have found

And what a jewel have I uncovered

No gold, nor silver, nor anything of brass

No diamond, no ruby, not even a shiny colored glass

None shall ever take the place of the jewel to which I

cling

For she is my love, my friend, my earthly everything!

Marriage

Isn't it worth the commitment of love
And knowing your vows are written above?

Isn't it worth having a partner for life
And being able to say, "That's my husband or wife"?

Isn't it worth the passionate kisses
And the fulfillment of anniversary wishes?

Isn't it worth the cuddles at night
And walks on the beach by the bright moonlight?

Isn't it worth the sweetheart names
And rekindling the fire of your passionate flame?

With these words, I humbly subdue
And with great conviction, I whisper to you

It is certainly worth hearing the words so true:
"With this ring, I thee wed, and I love you."

Poems from My Spirit

No Answer

What can a writer do but write?

A singer, but sing a song?

How can a pilot not take a flight?

The cook, not use the tongs?

Where can the soul find a false pleasure?

Or can the mind be put at ease with lies?

Can a pirate with dung replace his treasure?

The frugivorous his fruit with flies?

Would a foot be stable on quaking earth?

Or a hand grip pitch or slime?

Would an expectant mother desire stillbirth?

The aged, the swiftness of time?

Do we turn our eyes from the growth within?

Our hearts from delights not tasted?

Could life be better in endless chagrin?

Or with occasions of fulfillment gone wasted?

Reality

If life were like a fairy tale
You'd follow trails of bread grown stale
Placed in line to guide your path
So to know the way, you'd need not ask

If life were like a nursery rhyme
Your every step would pat in time
Its words would give a steady beat
In which to guide your walking feet

If life were like a sing-along
Your friends and kin would form a throng
A mighty throng and voice they'd be
To thwart the plans of your enemy

But life is simply real and true
Only God is able to guide you through
His Word is there to light your way
To reach His help, just kneel and pray.

Earth Time

I say, "I need it now."

But He says, "Wait."

I say, "Please be on time."

He says, "I'm never late."

I say, "Lord, when is it coming?"

But He says, "Be calm."

I say, "Time is winding up."

He says, "It won't be long."

I say, "Lord, I'm running out of time

And I'm down to my last dime."

But He says, "Be patient, my child—

Live by eternity, not by Earth Time."

I Wait for the Sound

The sound of my separation
What word can describe the glee?
God, He separates my sinful flesh from me

Does that even make a sound—
Changing from mortal to immortality?
I care not; please just set my spirit free

So grand a thing untouched by sound
To hear it, God, I'd give all to thee
But what shall I give, and what shall the price be?

I see and see and see
My flesh and sin, they both agree
I long, now until forever, to taste eternity

The sound of my separation
My ear aches to hear its beat
I wait, and I hear no sound; again, I wait tirelessly.

Death Becomes Me

Death becomes me
It fits like the mane of a full-grown lion
Yet it brings not the same glory
For I glory not in death
But death glories in its victory

Death becomes me
It embraces my flesh like the wedding band
Hugs the finger of the frail hand of a bride
Yet it brings not flutters of love
For I love not death
But death loves its victory

Death becomes me
We connect like man and woman
In the bonds of sanctified consummation
Yet it brings not life and birth
For I desire not to impregnate death
But death aborts the earth in victory

Death becomes me
Like a smile after a tickle

It's automatic, inevitable; it will come

Yet it brings not laughter and cheer

For I find no cheer in death

But death swallows laughter in victory.

Death becomes me

As the robe of the husbandman

And the garments of the sewer

Like the gown of the reaper, they

All receive the rewards of their work

Yet death brings not rewards of work

For I sew not, nor labor for death

But death collects a wage from me in victory

Death becomes me

Like the glorious sound of a trumpet

That lauds the sleeping kings of old

But like the trumpet, I shall cry aloud

Though death must come and bring desolation

God has come and will come again to bring life

For I have faith, and now I fear not death

I say death has no victory.

Memorialize Your Loved Ones

In Memory of Your Loved One

Your loved ones deserve to be remembered. What better way to honor and preserve their memory than to express, in your own words, who they were and what they meant to you and to the world? Poems are a unique way to do just that. However, any expression of remembrance is worth the time to be written and held as a memorial for the life of one that has passed on. I admonish you to take the time to bring to manifestation the nearest and dearest memories of those you love the most, whether they transitioned years ago or if you've recently experienced a loss. For your comfort and ease, pages have been provided to facilitate your own writing in loving memory of your loved one.

In Loving Memory of

_____

_____

In Loving Memory of

_____

_____

In Loving Memory
of

_____

_____

In Loving Memory of

_____

_____

_____

_____

_____

_____

_____

_____

_____

_____

_____

_____

_____

In Loving Memory
of

_____

_____

_____

_____

_____

_____

_____

_____

_____

_____

_____

_____

_____

In Loving Memory of

_____

_____

_____

_____

_____

_____

_____

_____

_____

_____

_____

_____

_____

_____

_____

About the Author

Dr. Calvin D. Franklin hails from a long heritage of church ministry and leadership. Several members of his ancestry were, and many family members are currently dedicated to the ministry of the Gospel of Jesus Christ through preaching, serving those in need, and comforting the bereaved. He follows in their footsteps at the leading of the Holy Spirit.

As he grew into adulthood, Dr. Calvin Franklin became more aware of the impact that everyday people have on the lives of just about everyone they know. That awareness and the desire to commemorate that impact for a coworker's father caused him to begin writing a special type of poetry. After presenting the bereaved family with the first elegy that he'd ever written, he decided to take advantage of the opportunity to continue expressing condolences for the loss of family, friends, and for the loved ones of others whom he may not have known himself. Experiencing a season of immense losses, Dr. Franklin intensified his writing as he was inspired to do so. As he wrote elegies, he also took the opportunity to write other poems and dedications by way of eulogies, special presentations, and parables.

Dr. Franklin has been recognized for his sincere and heartfelt poetry and has received acknowledgments for his work from Her Majesty, Queen Elizabeth II of England, the family of the late Reverend William "Billy" Graham, and from TV personality Ms. Robin René Roberts.

Dr. Franklin attributes his ability to communicate through the written word to God. Each time he is privileged with the opportunity to console a family, he carefully seeks the Lord in prayer and asks that he be given the right words. God has yet to fail him.

Dr. Franklin is a graduate of the William Preston Wiggins Bible College and is now a professor of theology. He serves as an associate elder at St. Paul Baptist Church in Virginia.

CPSIA information can be obtained
at www.ICGtesting.com
Printed in the USA
BVHW052256020622
638526BV00002B/7

9 781685 566296